DELICIOUS VEGETARIAN PIZZAS FOR EVERYBODY

Neil J Milliner

DELICIOUS VEGETARIAN PIZZAS FOR EVERYBODY

compiled by

Neil J Milliner

©2017

TABLE OF CONTENTS

not purchase it, or it was not purchased for your use only, then please return to your favorite ebook retailer and purchase your own copy. Thank you for respecting the hard work of this author.

For all your organic herbs,spices and oils. www.crueltyfreeorganics.net[1]

---

1. http://www.crueltyfreeorganics.net/

VEGETARIAN PIZZAS

Bertucci's Nolio Pizza Recipe

INGREDIENTS:

1 medium yellow onion

1 teaspoon white pepper

1 cup heavy cream

1/2 lemon

1 1/2 cup shredded mozzarella cheese

1 package pizza dough (or home made).

Olive oil.

Directions:

Preheat oven to 400º F.

Boil heavy cream until thickened.

Add white pepper and the juice from a half of a lemon.

Slice onion very thin so that you are left with rings.

Saute onion rings in olive oil until they are starting to get brown.

Assemble pizza as follows:

Unroll pizza dough onto a non-stick pizza pan.

Add cheese.

Add the cream mixture at a time to the pizza, a tablespoon at a time, forming little puddles spread around the pizza.

Drain the onions and put them on last. They will continue to caramelize as the pizza bakes.

Bake 8-10 minutes. Don't over bake. You don't want to "dry out" the pizza.

Butternut Squash And Rosemary Pizza Recipe

INGREDIENTS:

1 1/2 pound butternut squash

1 tablespoon vegetable oil

1/2 cup water

6 tablespoons unsalted butter, melted and kept warm

10 sheets phyllo stacked between sheets of wax paper and covered with a kitchen towel

9 tablespoons parmesan cheese—freshly grated

1 tablespoon fresh rosemary leaves—minced

6 scallion greens—chopped

1 small red onion sliced thin and separated into pieces

Directions:

Quarter squash lengthwise and discard seeds.

Peel squash carefully and cut into 3/4-inch pieces.

In a large heavy skillet cook squash in oil over moderate heat, stirring occasionally, 2 minutes.

Add water and salt to taste and simmer, covered, until squash is just tender, about 10 minutes.

Simmer squash, uncovered, until almost all water is evaporated, about 5 minutes.

In a food processor purée squash with salt and pepper to taste.

Squash purée may be made 1 day ahead and chilled, covered.

Preheat oven to 400°F.

Lightly brush a large baking sheet with some butter and put 1 sheet phyllo on butter. Lightly brush phyllo with some remaining butter and sprinkle with 1 tablespoon Parmesan.

Put another sheet of phyllo over cheese, pressing it firmly so that it adheres to bottom layer.

Butter, sprinkle with cheese, and layer remaining phyllo in the same manner, ending with a sheet of phyllo.

Lightly brush top sheet with remaining butter.

Fold in all sides 1/4 inch, pressing to top sheet, and fold up a 1/4-inch border, crimping corners.

Spread squash purée evenly on phyllo crust and top with rosemary, scallion greens, and onion.

Bake pizza in middle of oven until crust is golden, about 15 minutes.

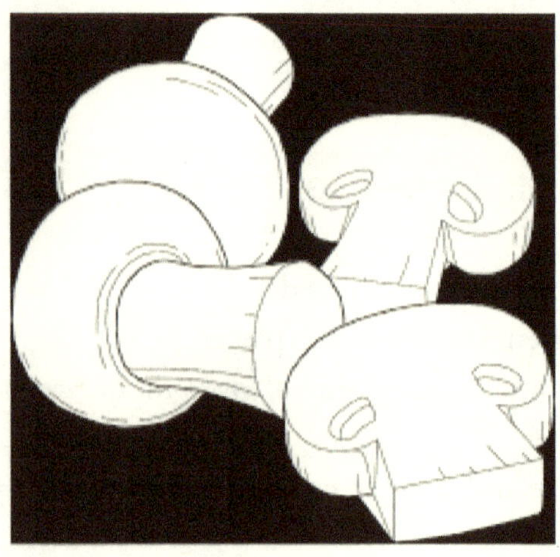

Caramelized Onion Pizza With Fontina Recipe

INGREDIENTS:

Pizza Dough

1 cup warm water (105 degrees)

1 1/4 ounce packet yeast

3 cups all-purpose flour

1 teaspoon salt

1 teaspoon sugar

2 tablespoons olive oil

Caramelized Onions

2 onions

2 teaspoons olive oil

1 1/2 teaspoon salt

1 1/2 cup coarsely grated fontina

1 clove garlic, cut in half

1 drizzle of olive oil. Salt and pepper to taste.

Directions:

Make the dough:

Pour the water into a large bowl.

Sprinkle in the yeast and sugar, and stir to dissolve.

Let it stand until the mixture begins to bubble. This should take about 5 minutes.

If the mixture doesn't bubble, start it over with another packet of yeast.

Stir in 1 cup of flour, the salt, and 1 tablespoon olive oil.

Mix with a wooden spoon until thoroughly incorporated.

Add the remaining flour 1/2 cup at a time, mixing after each addition.

On a lightly floured surface knead dough until smooth and elastic, about 10 minutes. Oil a large bowl with the remaining olive oil.

Place dough in oiled bowl, cover with plastic wrap and a warm dish towel, and let the dough rise in a warm place until doubled in bulk. This will take 1 to 1 1/2 hours.

Punch down the dough, and return it to the floured surface.

Divide dough into two balls and cover each with plastic wrap, leaving room for expansion.

Allow to double in size again.

Caramelized Onions:

Heat oil in large nonstick saute pan over medium heat.

Add thinly sliced onions and season with salt; saute 5 minutes.

Reduce heat to medium-low. Stir frequently to get an even color.

Cook until very tender and a rich golden color develops, about 20 minutes longer. Cool slightly.

Preheat oven to 475°F.

Roll out 2 dough disks on lightly floured surface to 8-inch rounds.

Sprinkle two baking sheets or pizza stones with cornmeal.

Rub a generous drizzle of olive oil on dough.

Rub raw garlic clove all over dough.

Top with fontina and caramelized onions

Season with salt and pepper.

Bake pizza for 10-12 minutes, until bubbling and crisp.

Cheesy Jalapeno And Egg Pizza Recipe

INGREDIENTS:

6 eggs

6 cups shredded cheddar cheese

6 cups shredded mozzarella cheese

6 ounces sliced jalapenos

Directions:

Mix eggs, cheese and jalapenos.

Pour into rectangular casserole.

Place into 350ºF oven.

Cook until cheese is golden (about 10-15 minutes).

Let stand for 5 minutes, cut into 2-inch squares and serve.

Easy Bake Oven Deep Dish Pizza Recipe

INGREDIENTS:

2 tablespoons all-purpose flour

1/8 teaspoon baking powder

Dash of salt

1 teaspoon butter

2 1/4 teaspoons milk

1 tablespoon pizza sauce

1 1/2 tablespoon shredded mozzarella cheese

Directions:

Stir together flour, baking powder, salt and butter until dough looks like medium-sized crumbs.

Slowly add milk while stirring.

Shape dough into a ball and place into a greased pan.

Use your fingers to pat the dough evenly over the bottom of the pan, then up the sides.

Pour the sauce evenly over the dough, then sprinkle with the cheese.

Bake at 400ºF for 20 minutes.

Fresh Tomato And Basil Pizza Recipe

INGREDIENTS:

1 (12") Italian bread shell like Boboli

1 tablespoon olive oil

1/2 cup grated or shredded Parmesan cheese, divided

3 plum tomatoes, sliced

1/4 teaspoon ground black pepper

2 tablespoons shredded fresh basil

Directions:

Preheat oven to 450ºF.

Brush bread shell with olive oil.

Sprinkle 1/4 cup of the cheese over the crust.

Top with tomato slices and remaining 1/4 cup cheese.

Sprinkle with pepper.

Bake directly on oven rack for 8-10 minutes or until crust is crisp and cheese is melted.

Sprinkle with basil before serving.

Gluten Free Rice Crust Pizza Recipe

INGREDIENTS:

Crust

2 1/2 cups cooked white rice

1/4 cup mozzarella cheese, grated

1 egg, lightly beaten

1/4 cup onion, finely chopped

1 clove garlic, minced

1 teaspoon olive oil

1 tablespoon butter, melted

Topping

1 cup tomato sauce or pizza sauce

1/2 teaspoon oregano or basil, dried

3/4 cup mozzarella cheese, grated

1/4 cup Parmesan or asiago cheese, grated

Directions:

Preheat oven to 425°F.

Mix the first four ingredients thoroughly.

Spread evenly on the bottom of a 12-inch pizza pan or pie pan.

Bake 15 minutes or until surface is lightly brown.

Saute onion and garlic in the olive oil.

Spread over the crust.

Spread on the pizza sauce; add dry herbs if the sauce is bland.

Sprinkle on the two kinds of cheese.

Return to the oven and bake for 8- 10 minutes until the sauce is bubbly and the cheese is melted.

Goat Cheese And Walnut Pizza Recipe

INGREDIENTS:

1 pizza crust

6 ounces fresh goat cheese

2 tablespoons walnut or safflower oil

1/2 cup walnuts

Directions:

Crumble the goat cheese and sprinkle it all over the pizza.

In a small bowl toss the walnuts with the walnut or safflower oil to coat.

Place the walnuts all over the pizza.

Place into 350°F oven.

Cook until cheese is golden (about 10-15 minutes).

Goat Cheese Pizza Recipe

INGREDIENTS:

1 large prefabricated pizza shell

7 ounces goat cheese, sliced thinly

2 cloves garlic minced

1 teaspoon dried basil

Olive oil for sprinkling

Directions:

Preheat oven to 450ºF.

Spread goat cheese on pizza shell

Sprinkle garlic, basil, salt and pepper over cheese

Spread out tomatoes and mushrooms

Sprinkle with olive oil

Let rest for five minutes before serving.

Individual Pesto Pizzas With Mushrooms And Olives Recipe

INGREDIENTS:

1/4 cup prepared pesto

8 baked individual pizza crusts

8 large spinach leaves, trimmed

1/2 cup pizza sauce

1/2 cup nonfat mozzarella cheese, shredded

6 small mushrooms, thinly sliced

5 black olives, thinly sliced

1 tablespoon parmesan cheese, freshly grated

Directions:

Preheat the oven to 400ºF.

Spray 1/2 tablespoon of the pesto on each of the pizza crusts.

Lay a spinach leaf on top and cover with 1 tablespoon of the pizza sauce.

Over the sauce, scatter 1 tablespoon of mozzarella cheese, then equal amounts of the sliced mushrooms and olives.

Finish with a light sprinkling of the parmesan cheese.

Place the pizzas on a cookie sheet and bake for 10 minutes.

Kid Sized Southwest Pizza Recipe

INGREDIENTS:

6 pita bread rounds

16 ounces can refried beans

4 ounces chopped green chilies drained

1/2 cup diced tomato

3/4 cup shredded cheese

1 1/2 cup shredded iceberg lettuce

6 tablespoons sour cream

Directions:

Preheat oven to 400ºF degrees.

Place pita rounds on a large greased baking sheet.

Bake 8 minutes or until crisp, turning after 4 minutes.

Let cool slightly.

Combine beans and chilies mixing well.

Spread about 1/3 cup bean mixture over each pita round.

Divide tomato evenly among pizzas.

Sprinkle with cheese.

Bake 8 minutes longer or until mixture is hot and cheese melts.

Remove from the oven.

Top each pizza with 1/4 cup lettuce and 1 tablespoon sour cream.

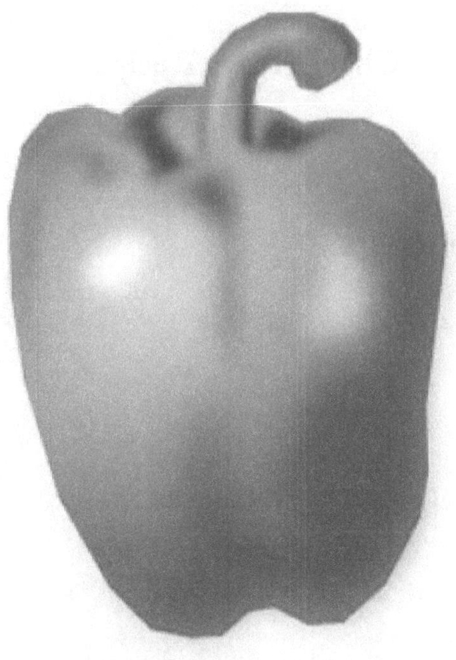

Leek, Tomato And Goat Cheese Pizza Recipe

INGREDIENTS:

1 1/2 tablespoon butter

2 med. leeks, thinly sliced

1 tablespoon fresh parsley, minced

3/4 cup tomato, chopped

3 ounces Montrachet or Feta, crumbled

2 tablespoons olive oil

Directions:

Melt butter in large skillet over medium-low heat.

Add leeks and saute until tender, about 10 minutes.

Season with salt and pepper.

Stir in parsley.

Cool.

Spread leek topping evenly over pizza shell and sprinkle tomatoes over.

Top with cheese.

Drizzle 1 tablespoon oil over.

Bake about 10 minutes at 450ºF.

Remove from oven and brush crust with olive oil.

Parsley Pesto And Feta Phyllo Pizza Recipe

INGREDIENTS:

Pesto

3 cups fresh parsley leaves—packed, rinsed and spun dry

2 cloves garlic cloves—chopped

1/3 cup parmesan cheese—freshly grated

1/3 cup pine nuts—toasted until golden and cooled

1/3 cup olive oil

6 tablespoons unsalted butter, melted and kept warm

10 sheets phyllo stacked between sheets of wax paper and covered with a kitchen towel

9 tablespoons parmesan cheese—freshly grated

3/4 cup crumbled feta cheese

Directions:

Preheat the oven to 400°F.

Make pesto:

In a food processor blend well all pesto ingredients.

Pesto may be made 3 days ahead and chilled, surface covered with plastic wrap.

Lightly brush a large baking sheet with some butter and put 1 sheet phyllo on butter. Lightly brush phyllo with some remaining butter and sprinkle with 1 tablespoon parmesan.

Put another sheet phyllo over cheese, pressing firmly so that it adheres to bottom layer.

Butter, sprinkle with cheese, and layer remaining phyllo in same manner, ending with a sheet of phyllo.

Lightly brush top sheet with remaining butter.

Fold in all sides 1/4 inch, pressing to top sheet, and fold up a 1/4-inch border, crimping corners.

Spread pesto and phyllo crust and sprinkle with feta.

Bake pizza in middle of oven until crust is golden, about 15 minutes.

Pita Pizza Recipe

INGREDIENTS:

1 ounce lowfat mozzarella cheese—shredded

1 pita bread

sun-dried tomato halves—rehydrated with water and chopped

1 marinated artichoke heart—rinsed and drained

chopped or sliced fresh basil

red pepper—hot or mild, fresh or roasted

Directions:

Shred low-fat mozzarella onto pita round

Add sun-dried tomatoes, marinated artichoke heart, snips of fresh basil and bottled red pepper or, thinly slice a fresh red pepper.

Broil until hot and bubbly.

Pizza Arizona Recipe

INGREDIENTS:

2 teaspoons yellow cornmeal

1 (10-ounce) tube refrigerated pizza dough

1 1/2 cup purchased chipotle salsa

2 tablespoons olive oil

1 1/2 teaspoon chili powder

1 1/2 cup shredded Mexican-style four-cheese mix or pizza cheese

1/4 cup chopped fresh cilantro

Directions:

Position rack in bottom third of oven and preheat to 400°F.

Sprinkle cornmeal on baking sheet.

Unroll dough onto sheet, forming 10x15-inch rectangle.

Mix salsa, oil, and chili powder in small bowl.

Toss cheese and cilantro in medium bowl.

Spoon salsa mixture over dough, leaving 1/2-inch border.

Sprinkle with cheese mixture.

Bake pizza until crust is golden brown and cheese is melted and bubbling, about 15 minutes.

Cut into squares and serve.

Pizza For Easybake Oven Recipe

INGREDIENTS:

2 tablespoons all-purpose flour

1/8 teaspoon baking powder

1 dash salt

1 teaspoon butter

2 1/4 teaspoons milk

1 tablespoon pizza sauce

1 1/2 tablespoon shredded mozzarella cheese

Directions:

Stir together flour, baking powder, salt and butter until dough looks like medium-sized crumbs.

Slowly add milk while stirring.

Shape dough into a ball and place into a greased pan.

Use your fingers to pat the dough evenly over the bottom of the pan, then up the sides.

Pour the sauce evenly over the dough, then sprinkle with the cheese.

Bake at about 400ºF for 20 minutes.

Pizza Pesto Verde Recipe

INGREDIENTS:

1 (12- or 14-inch size) pizza crust

2 cups mozzarella, shredded

1 cup feta, crumbled

1 cup prepared pesto sauce

1 cup spinach, chopped

1 cup canned tomatoes, diced and drained

Directions:

Preheat oven to 425ºF.

Spread pesto sauce on partially baked crust and top with chopped spinach.

Sprinkle mozzarella evenly over sauce, then top with tomatoes and feta.

Bake about 15 minutes, or until the mozzarella is melted and the crust is crisp and golden.

Pizza Rice Cakes Recipe

INGREDIENTS:

4 Rice cakes

1/3 cup Pizza sauce

1/4 cup Sliced ripe olives

1/4 cup Diced green pepper

1/4 cup Sliced mushrooms

1/3 cup Shredded mozzarella cheese

Directions:

Place rice cakes on baking sheet.

Spread pizza auce evenly on each rice cake and top with remaining ingredients.

Bake at 400ºF degrees for 10 minutes.

Pizza Santa Fe Style Recipe

INGREDIENTS:

1 (12-inch) pizza crust, ready to bake

Sauce

1 1/2 cup lightly packed cilantro leaves

1/2 cup lightly packed parsley leaves

2 cloves garlic

1 jalapeno chile, halved, seeded

1 scallion, cut in pieces

1 tablespoon lemon juice

1/2 cup olive oil

salt and freshly ground pepper to taste

Topping

2 Anaheim or mild green chiles, roasted, peeled, seeded, cut into strips

5 tomatillos (or substitute green tomatoes), husked, rinsed, sliced

4 small plum tomatoes, sliced and drained on paper towels

1 small red onion, thinly sliced

salt and freshly ground pepper

1 tablespoon chopped fresh oregano or 1/2 teaspoon dried

2 cups grated jack cheese

Directions:

Combine all sauce ingredients except salt and pepper in a food processor or blender. Puree until smooth.

Add salt and pepper to taste.

Preheat oven to 450°F.

Place pizza crust on a large baking sheet.

Brush the shell with the sauce.

Arrange strips of chiles, radiating out from the center.

Arrange slices of tomatillos, tomatoes, and red onions in between.

Sprinkle with salt and pepper and oregano.

Top with grated cheese and bake for 5 to 10 minutes, until edges are crisp, and serve hot.

Pizza With Fontina, Artichoke Hearts And Red Onion Recipe

INGREDIENTS:

1 pound frozen white bread dough; thawed according to package directions

2 tablespoons olive oil; divided

2 tablespoons wheat bran or cornmeal

1 clove garlic; chopped finely

1/2 medium red onion; thinly sliced

1 package (9 oz. size) frozen artichokes; thawed

Salt

Freshly ground black pepper

1 cup shredded Fontina cheese

Directions:

Drain and slice artichoke hearts.

Preheat oven to 450ºF.

On lightly oiled baking sheet, press chilled dough into 9 x 12 inch rectangle, crimp edges to form a rim.

Brush with half the oil.

Evenly sprinkle with bran or cornmeal and press lightly into dough.

Sprinkle with garlic.

Arrange onion in 1 layer over dough and top with artichoke hearts.

Drizzle with the remaining oil.

Lightly season with salt and pepper.

Evenly sprinkle with cheese.

Do not let dough rise.

The pizza may be held briefly in the refrigerator before baking.

Bake 15 minutes or until crust is golden brown.

Polenta Pizzarina Recipe

INGREDIENTS:

2 quarts water

2 cups polenta

16 ounces soy mozzarella cheese

1/2 teaspoon dried chili pepper flakes

1/2 cup vegetarian pizza sauce

2 large, not-quite-ripe tomatoes, rinsed

1 large green pepper, rinsed and de-seeded

12 ounces box mushrooms, wiped clean

1 tablespoon Italian or pizza seasoning

Non-fat cooking spray

Directions:

Preheat oven to 350°F.

Put water in a large pot or Dutch oven and bring to a boil over high heat.

Meanwhile grate the soy cheese and set aside.

When water is boiling, slowly pour in the polenta while stirring at the same time. Reduce heat to medium-low and continue stirring the polentaevery few minutes to avoid lumps and prevent schorching. You may want to partially cover the pot with a lid as the polenta tends to start spitting as it thickens.It should take about 20 minutes for the polenta to become as thick as porridge.

In the meantime, finely chop the green pepper and slice the mushrooms and tomatoes. Heat some non-fat cooking spray in a frying pan, add peppers and mushrooms and saute a few minutes over medium heat until the juices have been released. Drain off excess juice.

When the polenta has thickened, turn off heat and stir in half of the grated soy mozzarella and all of the dried pepper flakes.

Transfer the polenta to a 10" by 15" rectangular glass or stainless steel oven pan and spread out evenly.

Let cool for 15 minutes while you take a break.

When the polenta has sufficiently cooled, spread the pizza sauce evenly over the top, followed by the tomato slices, green peppers and mushrooms.

Sprinkle remainder of the soy mozzarella on top of the vegetables, followed by the Italian seasoning.

Place dish in oven on lower rack and bake 15-20 minutes until heated through and cheese has melted.

Crispy Sweet Onion Pizza Recipe

INGREDIENTS:

1 (12-inch) prebaked pizza shell

2 1/2 tablespoons olive oil

1 pound sweet onions halved, sliced vertically

1/4 cup sun-dried tomatoes (packed in oil), chopped

1/2 teaspoon dried oregano

1/2 teaspoon dried thyme

1/2 teaspoon dried basil

Salt and pepper to taste

Directions:

Heat oven to 425ºF.

Place pizza shell on baking sheet and sprinkle onions on pizza and drizzle with olive oil.

Top with sun-dried tomatoes.

Sprinkle with herbs, salt and pepper.

Bake until onions just begin to brown, about 10 minutes.

Spa Pizzas Recipe

INGREDIENTS:

3 tablespoons olive oil

1/2 cup minced onions

1 cup tomato sauce

1/2 teaspoon oregano

1/4 teaspoon Italian seasoning

3/4 cup sliced mushrooms

1/2 medium zucchini, thinly sliced

1/2 cup diced red pepper

4 (8-inch) flour or (6-inch) corn tortillas

1/2 cup black olives

1 cup grated mozzarella cheese

1/2 cup diced green pepper

Directions:

Heat 2 Tbsp. oil in a heavy medium saucepan over medium heat.

Add onions & cook until golden, stirring occasionally, about 5 minutes.

Stir in tomato sauce, garlic, oregano & Italian seasoning.

Simmer until thickened, about five minutes.

Heat remaining 1 Tbsp. oil in skillet over medium deat.

Add mushrooms & zucchini & cook until tender, stirring occasionally, about five minutes.

Set aside.

Preheat oven to 350°F.

Place tortillas on baking sheet & bake until crisp, about 4 minutes.

Spread about 1/4 cup sauce over each.

Sprinkle each with 1/4 cup cheese.

Top pizzas with mushrooms, zucchini, peppers & olives.

Bake until cheese melts, about 5 minutes.

Serve.

Spinach And Goat Cheese French Bread Pizzas Recipe

INGREDIENTS:

2 cups torn spinach

Vegetable cooking spray

1/8 teaspoon pepper

1 French roll; (7-inch-long)

1/4 cup tomato paste

1/4 teaspoon dried Italian seasoning

1/2 clove garlic ; minced

1 Hard-cooked egg; sliced

2 tablespoons crumbled chevre (goat cheese)

Directions:

Place spinach in a large nonstick skillet coated with cooking spray, cover and cook over low heat 7 minutes or until spinach wilts, stirring occasionally.

Toss with pepper, and set aside.

Slice roll in half lengthwise then place those, cut sides up, on a baking sheet.

Broil 2 minutes or until golden.

Combine tomato paste, Italian seasoning, and garlicand stir well, and spread this over the cut sides of bread.

Top with spinach mixture, egg, and cheese.

Broil 2 minutes or until cheese softens.

Three Cheese Pizza With Mushrooms And Basil Recipe

INGREDIENTS:

Cooking spray

1 (8-ounce) package pre-sliced mushrooms

1/2 cup part-skim ricotta cheese

1/4 cup shredded fresh Parmesan cheese

1 (10-ounce) Italian cheese-flavored pizza crust (such as Boboli)

1 cup chunky vegetable pasta sauce

1/2 cup shredded part-skim mozzarella cheese

2 tablespoons thinly-sliced fresh basil

Directions:

Preheat oven to 450ºF.

Heat a large nonstick skillet coated with cooking spray over medium-high heat.

Add mushrooms; sauté 5 minutes.

Remove from heat.

Combine ricotta and Parmesan cheeses.

Place pizza crust on a baking sheet.

Spread pasta sauce over crust, leaving a 1-inch border.

Dollop ricotta cheese mixture evenly over sauce and top with mushrooms.

Sprinkle with mozzarella.

Bake 12 minutes or until crust is crisp.

Sprinkle with basil; cut into wedges.

Truffle Pizza Recipe

INGREDIENTS:

1 tablespoon yeast

1 cup warm water (110ºF)

1/4 cup olive oil

3 1/2 cups flour

2 teaspoons salt

1 pound new potatoes; thinly sliced, blanched

1 cup julienned red onions

2 tablespoons extra-virgin olive oil

Salt to taste

Freshly-ground white pepper to taste

1/2 cup grated Parmigiano-Regginao cheese

1 drizzle truffle oil

2 tablespoons chopped chives

Directions:

Preheat the oven 400ºF.

In an electric mixer, whisk the yeast, water, and oil, together, to form a paste.

Using a dough hook, add the flour and salt to the paste, mix the dough until the dough comes away from the sides and crawls up the sides of the hook.

Remove the dough from the bowl and turn the dough into a greased bowl, cover.

Let the dough rise until double in size, about 1 hour.

Turn the dough out onto a floured surface and divide into four 4-ounce balls, cover. Let the dough rest for 10 to 15 minutes.

Press each dough out into a 10-inch circle about 1/2- to 1-inch thick.

Lightly brush the dough with olive oil.

Divide the potatoes into four portions and season with salt and pepper.

Cover each dough with the potatoes, leaving a 1-inch border.

In a small mixing bowl, toss the red onions with the extra- virgin olive oil.

Season with salt and pepper.

Place a layer of the red onions on top of the potatoes.

Sprinkle each pizza with the grated cheese.

Drizzle each pizza with the truffle oil.

Bake for 15 to 20 minutes or until the crust is crispy and golden-brown.

Garnish the pizza with chives.

White Onion Pizza Recipe

INGREDIENTS:

1 recipe pizza dough

3 medium onions

1/4 cup grated Romano cheese

1/2 cup grated/shredded other white cheese such as mozzarella, white cheddar etc

2 tablespoons extra virgin olive oil

3 tablespoons chopped parsley

Salt, pepper, garlic powder, dried: oregano, basil, thyme to taste

Directions:

No tomato sauce for this pizza, hence "'white" pizza.

Good quality olive oil as well as cheeses are important for best flavor and quality. Peel whole onions and boil 5 minutes and drain.

When cool, slice thin and rinse under water and drain again.

Roll out dough and place on pizza pan or warm oven stone.

Sprinkle with olive oil and spread over onions.

Sprinkle on cheeses and season to taste with salt, pepper and herbs.

Bake in a preheated 450ºF oven about 20 to 25 minutes.

Sprinkle on parsley.

Cool 5 minutes before slicing.

Slice into 6 to 8 pieces or as desired.

Serve with a green salad , and a glass of wine for dinner!

White Pizza Recipe

INGREDIENTS:

1 pizza shell, 12"

2 tablespoons olive oil

4 teaspoons garlic; chopped fine

2 tablespoons basil, fresh; OR

2 teaspoons basil, dried

2 medium tomato; thinly sliced

1/4 pound mozzarella; grated, or to-taste

1/4 pound provolone; grated, or to-taste

1/4 cup Romano; grated

2 teaspoons oregano, dried

Directions:

Roll crust out to 12" circle.

Brush crust with olive oil, sprinkle with garlic and basil.

Arrange tomato slices over crust and top with grated mozzarella, provolone, and Romano cheeses.

Bake in a hot preheated oven (425ºF to 450ºF) 12 to 15 minutes or until cheese has melted and crust is lightly browned.

Sprinkle with oregano.

For best results, bake on parchment paper directly on pizza stone or oven tiles

White Pizza with Mascarpone and Smoked Mozzarella Recipe

INGREDIENTS:

8 ounces grated smoked mozzarella

1 teaspoon chopped fresh thyme

or

1/2 teaspoon dried thyme

1 teaspoon chopped fresh oregano

or

1/2 teaspoon dried oregano

2 garlic cloves

1/2 cup ricotta cheese

1/4 cup mascarpone

Salt and freshly ground black pepper

1 large Boboli pizza shell or similar

1 tablespoon olive oil

Directions:

Preheat the oven to 450°F.

Grate the smoked mozzarella.

If using fresh herbs, chop enough thyme and oregano to measure 1 teaspoon each.

Chop the 2 garlic cloves.

In a small bowl, blend the 1/2 cup ricotta and 1/4 cup mascarpone together well and season with salt and plenty of ground black pepper.

Place the pizza shell on a large baking pan and brush it with the 1 tablespoon olive oil.

With a spatula, spread the ricotta mixture evenly over the shell.

Sprinkle the grated smoked mozzarella over the top, then scatter the 1 teaspoon each of fresh herbs and the 2 chopped garlic cloves over the mozzarella.

Bake the pizza for 15 minutes, or until hot and bubbly.

Remove the pizza from the oven and let it rest a minute of two before cutting into wedges.

White Spinach Pizza Recipe

INGREDIENTS:

1 (10-oz) can refrigerated pizza crust

1 cup skim milk

3 tablespoons all-purpose flour

Salt and pepper to taste

1/2 pound mushrooms, sliced

1/2 teaspoon minced garlic

3 cups fresh spinach, washed and stemmed

1/2 teaspoon dried basil

1/4 cup crumbled feta

1/2 cup shredded part-skim mozzarella cheese

Directions:

Preheat oven to 425°F.

Pat crust into a round 12-inch pizza pan coated with nonstick cooking spray.

Bake for 7 minutes or until crust begins to brown.

In a small pot, mix together milk and flour over medium-high heat until thickened. Season with salt and pepper to taste.

Spread white sauce over partially baked crust.

Meanwhile, in a skillet coated with nonstick cooking spray, sauté mushrooms and garlic until tender, about 5 minutes.

Add spinach, stirring until wilted.

Add basil.

Spread spinach mixture over white sauce.

Sprinkle with feta and mozzarella cheeses.

Return to oven and continue baking for 10 minutes until crust is golden brown and cheese is melted.

Windy City Pizza Recipe

INGREDIENTS:

1 1/2 package refrigerated crescent rolls

8 ounces cream cheese, softened

1/4 cup fresh Parmesan cheese, grated

1 small garlic clove, pressed

2 plum tomatoes, thinly sliced

1/4 cup green bell pepper, chopped

1 tablespoon fresh basil leaves, snipped

Directions:

Preheat oven to 350°F.

Unroll dough and divide into triangles.

Roll or press crescent rolls together on a round or rectangle pizza pan or cookie sheet. Bake at 350° for 12-15 minutes or until golden brown.

Cool completely.

Mix cream cheese, garlic and 1 tablespoons of Parmesan cheese.

Spread evenly over crust.

Top with tomato slices, chopped green pepper and green onions.

Deep Dish Mexican Pizza Recipe

INGREDIENTS:

1 thick pizza crust

nonstick cooking spray

1/2 small onion—diced

1 teaspoon chili powder

1/2 teaspoon ground cumin

1/4 teaspoon ground cinnamon

15 ounces black beans—rinsed and drained

2 ounces diced green chilies

cornmeal

1 cup shredded monterey jack cheese

3/4 cup diced tomatoes

1/2 cup frozen whole kernel corn—thawed

1/2 green bell pepper—diced

2 ounces sliced ripe black olives—drained

1/2 teaspoon olive oil

Salsa—optional

Sour cream—optional

Directions:

Prepare Pizza Crust.

Preheat oven to 500°F.

Spray 2- to 3-quart saucepan with cooking spray.

Place over medium heat.

Add onion, chili powder, cumin, cinnamon and 1 tablespoon water and stir.

Cover and cook 3 to 4 minutes or until onion is crisp-tender.

Stir in beans and chilies.

Transfer 1/2 of the bean mixture to food processor or blender then process until almost smooth.

Spray 14-inch deep-dish pizza pan with nonstick cooking sprayand sprinkle with cornmeal.

Press dough gently into bottom and up side of pan.

Cover with plastic wrap and let stand in warm place 15 to 20 minutes or until puffy. Bake 5 to 7 minutes or until dry and firm on top.

Spread pureed bean mixture over crust up to thick edge.

Top with half the cheese, the remaining bean mixture, tomatoes, corn, bell pepper and olives.

Top with remaining cheese.

Bake 10 to 12 minutes more or until crust is deep golden.

Brush crust edges with olive oil.

Cut into wedges.

Serve with salsa and sour cream.

Mayonnaise Burrito Pizzas Recipe

INGREDIENTS:

4 flour tortillas

8 ounces catsup

8 ounces freshly squeezed mayonnaise

8 ounces American cheese

8 ounces cheddar cheese

Directions:

Preheat oven to 350°F.

Arrange the tortillas on cookie sheet.

Mix catsup and mayonnaise in bowl, divide into 4 portions, spread each portion onto each tortilla.

Top with cheese, half American and half cheddar.

Cook 15-20 minutes.

Serve.

Mexican Pita Pizzas Recipe

INGREDIENTS:

4 Pita breads

1 can black beans (15 oz) drained

1 can Pico de Gallo (11.5 oz) drained

1 cup cheese, Cheddar shredded

1 cup cheese, Monterey Jack shredded

2 cups lettuce shredded

Salsa

Guacamole

Scallions sliced

Olives, ripe

Sliced

Directions:

Heat oven to 375°F.

Place pita breads on large baking sheet.

In medium bowl, combine beans and Pico de Gallo.

Spoon over pita breads.

Sprinkle each with cheeses.

Bake 14 to 18 minutes or until heated through and cheese is melted.

Top with shredded lettuce.

Cut each into 6 wedges.

Serve with salsa, sour cream, guacamole, scallions and/or olives.

Mexican Pizza Recipe

INGREDIENTS:

For dough

1 cup warm water

2 tablespoons warm water

2 1/2 teaspoons active dry yeast

1/2 teaspoon sugar

3 tablespoons peanut oil

2 1/3 cups all-purpose flour

2/3 cup cornmeal plus additional for sprinkling pizza pan

1 teaspoon salt

1/2 teaspoon ground cumin

For sauce

1 1/2 pound fresh tomatillos, husks discarded

1 small onion, sliced thin

2 garlic cloves, sliced thin

2 tablespoons peanut oil

1/4 cup packed fresh coriander sprigs, washed, dried, and chopped

1 tablespoon fresh lime juice

1 1/2 cup grated Mexican blend cheese or cheddar

2 fresh poblano chilies, roasted and cut into thin strips

2 scallions, sliced thin

1/4 cup thinly sliced drained pimento-stuffed green olives

1/4 cup cooked black beans, rinsed if canned

Directions:

Make dough:

In a small saucepan heat 1/2 cup water to 110°F. and transfer to a large bowl.

Stir in yeast and sugar and let stand 5 minutes, or until foamy.

Stir in remaining water and dough ingredients to form a dough and on a lightly floured surface knead until smooth and elastic, about 10 minutes.

Put dough in a lightly oiled deep bowl, turning to coat, and let rise, covered loosely, in a warm place until doubled in bulk, about 1 hour. (Alternatively, let dough rise, covered loosely, in refrigerator overnight, or until doubled in bulk.)

Make sauce:

In a 4-quart saucepan of boiling water blanch tomatillos 1 minute and drain in a colander.

Cut each tomatillo into 8 wedges.

In a large heavy skillet cook onion and garlic in oil over moderate heat, stirring occasionally, until onion is pale golden.

Add tomatillos and cook over moderate heat, stirring occasionally, until tomatillos are softened and mixture is reduced to about 1 1/4 cups.

Cool mixture slightly and in a food processor purée until smooth.

Transfer sauce to a bowl and stir in coriander, lime juice, and salt to taste.

Preheat oven to 525°F. and adjust oven rack on top shelf.

Sprinkle a 16-inch perforated pizza pan with additonal cornmeal.

Punch down dough and on a lightly floured work surface with a floured rolling pin roll out into a 17-inch circle.

Fit dough into pan, forming an edge, and bake 5minutes.

Spread sauce over partially cooked dough, leaving a 1/2-inch border around edge, and sprinkle with cheese, chilies, scallions, olives, and beans.

Bake pizza 10 minutes, or until cheese is melted and crust is pale golden.

To Roast Peppers:

Using a long-handled fork char the peppers over an open flame, turning them, for 2 to 3 minutes, or until the skins are blackened. (Or broil the peppers on the rack of a broiler pan under a preheated broiler about 2 inches from the heat, turning them every 5 minutes, for 15 to 25 minutes, or until the skins are blistered and charred.)

Transfer the peppers to a bowl and let them steam, covered, until they are cool enough to handle.

Keeping the peppers whole, peel them starting at the blossom end, cut off the tops, and discard the seeds and ribs.

Mexican Pizza Recipe 2

INGREDIENTS:

1 (12" size) pre-baked pizza/bread crust

1 can spicy refried beans (16 oz. size)

3/4 cup medium salsa

1/2 cup cheddar cheese—shredded

1/2 cup monterey jack cheese—shredded

1/2 cup green onions—sliced

1 can sliced black olives—drained (2 1/4 oz. size)

1 teaspoon cilantro—minced

Directions:

Place crust on large baking sheet.

In a bowl, combine beans and salsa then spread on crust.

Sprinkle on remaining ingredients except cilantro.

Bake at 450ºF for 10 minutes.

Top with cilantro.

Mexican Stuffed Pizza Recipe

INGREDIENTS:

1 can (15 oz.) chili with beans

1 can (4 oz.) diced green chiles

2 packages (8 oz.) refrigerated crescent roll dough

1/2 cup shredded cheddar cheese

2 cups toppings (shredded lettuce, chopped tomato, sliced
ripe olives, chopped onions, guacamole, sour cream
and shredded cheddar cheese)

Directions:

Preheat oven to 350°F.

Combine chili and green chiles in medium bowl.

Slightly overlap crescent dough triangles around edge of 10-to 12-inch-round pizza pan, positioning top half of each triangle so that it is hanging over the edge of the pan.

Spoon chili mixture in center of each crescent roll triangle then bring the top half of each triangle over chili and tuck under pointed end.

Sprinkle with cheese.

Bake for 30 to 35 minutes at 350°F or until golden brown.

Top immediately with toppings.

Serve hot.

Artichoke And Red Pepper Pizza Recipe

INGREDIENTS:

1 pizza shell
1 tablespoon olive oil
1 cup julienne cut red bell pepper
1 teaspoon dried basil
1 teaspoon dried oregano
5 garlic cloves, minced
1 can artichoke hearts, drained and chopped (not in oil)
1 jar sliced mushrooms, drained
1 1/2 cup shredded part skim mozzarella cheese
Freshly cracked pepper

Directions:

Heat oil in a nonstick skillet, simmer ingredients until tender.
Place on boboli shell and top with cheese.
Bake at the directions given on the Boboli package.

Artichoke Pepper Pizza Recipe

INGREDIENTS:

1 medium red bell pepper

1 teaspoon olive oil

2 cloves garlic, crushed

1/4 cup light mayonnaise

1/8 teaspoon red pepper

1/8 teaspoon black pepper

1 cup artichoke hearts

1 (1-pound size) cooked pizza crust (like Boboli)

1 cup shredded mozzarella cheese

1/2 cup crumbled feta cheese

1/2 teaspoon thyme

Directions:

Cut the red bell pepper into strips.

Saute in the olive oil in a skillet for 3 minutes.

Stir in half the garlic.

Saute for 1 minute.

Process the remaining garlic, mayonnaise, red pepper, black pepper and artichokes in a food processor until the artichokes are finely chopped.

Place the pizza crust on a baking sheet.

Spread with the artichoke mixture to within 1/2 inch of the edge.

Top with the red bell pepper.

Sprinkle with the mozzarella cheese, feta cheese and thyme.

Bake at 450°F for 14 minutes.

Avocado And Everything Pizza Recipe

INGREDIENTS:

2 cups buttermilk baking mix

1/2 cup hot water

1 can (8 ounces) tomato sauce

1/4 cup chopped green onion

1/2 cup shredded mozzarella cheese

1/2 cup sliced mushrooms

1/3 cup sliced ripe olives

1 small tomato, sliced

2 tablespoons olive oil

1 avocado, seeded, peeled and sliced

Fresh basil leaves, optional

Directions:

Heat oven to 425°F.

Stir together buttermilk mix and water with fork in small bowl.

Pat or roll into 12-inch circle on ungreased baking sheet or pizza pan.

Mix together tomato sauce and green onion and spread over pizza dough.

Top with cheese, mushrooms, olives and tomato slices.

Drizzle olive oil over top.

Bake 15 to 20 minutes or until edge of crust is golden brown.

Remove pizza from oven and arrange avocado slices over top.

Garnish with basil leaves and serve.

Bell Pepper, Red Onion, And Goat Cheese Pizza Recipe

INGREDIENTS:

1 (10-ounce size) fully baked thin pizza crust (such as Boboli)

1/4 cup olive oil

3 cloves garlic, minced

3 cups (packed) baby spinach leaves

1 1/2 cup thickly sliced mushrooms

1/2 cup drained roasted red peppers from jar, cut into thin strips

1/2 cup paper-thin red onion slices

8 large fresh basil leaves, cut into thin strips

1 package (5-ounce size) soft fresh goat cheese, coarsely crumbled (or mozzarella, fontina, gorgonzola)

Directions:

Preheat oven to 425ºF.

Place pizza crust on large baking sheet.

Mix olive oil and minced garlic in small bowl.

Using pastry brush, brush 2 tablespoons garlic oil evenly over crust.

Top with spinach leaves, then sprinkle with sliced mushrooms, roasted red peppers, red onion slices, fresh basil, and crumbled goat cheese.

Drizzle pizza evenly with remaining garlic oil.

Bake pizza until crust is crisp and cheese begins to brown, about 18 minutes.

Transfer pizza to board.

Cut into wedges and serve warm.

Better Than Frozen French Bread Pizza Recipe

INGREDIENTS:

1 loaf crusty French bread

or

2 individual submarine-style hard rolls, split lengthwise

3/4 cup prepared low fat chunky or garden style spaghetti sauce

1 teaspoon dried oregano

1/2 fresh green pepper, sliced thinly

1/2 cup fresh or canned mushrooms, thinly sliced

1/4 cup fat-free parmesan cheese

1 cup low fat, shredded mozzarella cheese

Directions:

Spoon spaghetti sauce over sliced bread or rolls.

Top with mushrooms and green peppers.

Sprinkle with oregano and cheeses.

Bake in 350°F preheated oven for 12-15 minutes.

Black And White Pizza Recipe

INGREDIENTS:

1 loaf frozen bread dough—thawed

3 large onions—sliced thin

3 tablespoons olive oil

1 1/2 teaspoon dried sweet basil

Dash seasoned Salt

16 ounces black olives—drained & sliced

8 ounces mozzarella cheese—shredded

Directions:

Follow package directions for thawing bread dough.

In a large skillet heat oil, reduce heat then add the onions.

Cover and cook, stirring frequently, until onions are just tender.

Stir in seasoning and basil.

Grease a cookie sheet and set aside.

Roll dough into an 11 x 14 rectangle on a lightly floured surface.

Carefully lift dough onto cookie sheet.

Gently spread onions and cheese over dough leaving an edge.

Sprinkle on olives.

Let this rest 15 minutes.

Heat oven to 425°F degrees.

Bake 15 minutes or until crust is golden brown.

Broccoli Mushroom Pizza Recipe

INGREDIENTS:

1 tablespoon olive oil

2 cups sliced fresh mushrooms

1 medium onion—chopped

10 ounces frozen chopped broccoli—thawed and drained

1 cup spaghetti sauce

1 prepared pizza crust

8 ounces shredded mozzarella cheese

Directions:

Preheat the oven to 400°F.

Grease a pizza pan or baking sheet.

Saute the onions and mushrooms in the olive oil in a large skillet until soft.

Stir in the broccoli and cook until liquid is evaporated.

Stir in spaghetti sauce then remove from heat.

Spoon sauce onto prepared pizza crust, leaving about one inch around the perimeter. Top evenly with cheese.

Bake for 15 minutes or until cheese is melted and crust is golden.

Broccoli Pizza Recipe

INGREDIENTS:

1 tablespoon olive oil

1 clove garlic, minced

1 (12-inch) pizza crust

1 package (8 oz) shredded mozzarella cheese, divided

1 cup small broccoli flowerets

1/2 cup thin red onion wedges,

1/2 cup sliced yellow squash

1/2 cup red pepper strips

1 tablespoon dried oregano leaves

Directions:

Preheat oven to 450ºF.

Mix oil and garlic and brush on pizza crust.

Top with 1 cup cheese, broccoli, onion, squash, red pepper, remaining 1 cup cheese and oregano.

Bake 8-10 minutes or until cheese is melted.

Broccoli, Rabe And Chick-Pea Pita Pizza Recipe

INGREDIENTS:

2 cloves garlic—sliced thinly

1/4 cup extra-virgin olive oil

1 (19-ounce) can chick-peas—rinsed and drained

1/2 cup water

1 large bunch broccoli rabe, chopped, coarse stems discarded

1/2 teaspoon dried hot red pepper flakes

3 (6-inch) pita breads split in half to form circles

1/2 cup parmesan cheese—freshly grated

Directions:

Preheat oven to 400°F.

In a large heavy skillet cook garlic in oil over moderate heat, stirring, until pale golden.

Transfer garlic and 1 tablespoon oil to a food processor.

Add chick-peas, 1/4 cup water, and salt and pepper to taste and blend mixture until smooth.

Heat remaining oil in a skillet over moderately high heat until hot but not smoking and cook broccoli rabe, turning it with tongs, until wilted.

Add remaining 1/4 cup water and pepper flakes and simmer, covered partially, until broccoli rabe is crisp-tender and almost all liquid is evaporated, about 2 minutes.

Spread inside sides of pita with chick-pea purée and top with broccoli rabe and Parmesan.

Arrange pita pizzas on a large baking sheet and bake in middle of oven 10 minutes, or until edges are golden.

Cabbage Pizza Recipe

INGREDIENTS:

1 onion—minced

3 cloves garlic—minced

2 tablespoons oil

4 cups chopped cabbage

1 tablespoon fennel seed

1 cup tomato sauce

1/2 cup Parmesan cheese—freshly grated

1 prepared whole wheat pizza crust

Directions:

In a frying pan, saute, the onion and garlic in the oil for 5 minutes, or until soft.

Add the cabbage and fennel seeds, stir well, and cover.

Cook over medium-low heat until the cabbage is just wilted.

Preheat the oven to 425ºF.

Place the pizza crust on a greased baking sheet, and top with the tomato sauce, then the cabbage mixture.

Sprinkle with the Parmesan cheese.

Bake for 15 to 20 minutes,or until the cheese is lightly browned.

California Pizza Kitchen Grilled Eggplant Cheeseless Pizza Recipe

INGREDIENTS:

3 Tbsp olive oil, divided

1/2 teaspoon soy sauce

1/4 teaspoon cumin

1 pinch cayenne pepper

4 Japanese eggplants, sliced lengthwise 1/8-in. thick

Pizza dough as needed

2/3 cup red onion, sliced in 1/8-in. rings

2 tablespoons fresh cilantro, chopped

4 cups fresh spinach, cut in 1/4-in. strips

6 oil-packed, sun-dried tomatoes, drained, patted dry, julienned

Extra-virgin olive oil optional

Balsamic vinegar optional

Directions:

Combine 1 Tbsp. olive oil, soy sauce, cumin and cayenne.

Lightly coat both sides of eggplant slices with mixture.

Discard outside skin-covered slices.

Grill eggplant 2 to 3 minutes per side and set aside.

Shape pizza dough into 2 9-inch rounds.

Brush each with 1 Tbsp. olive oil.

Layer with onions then grilled eggplant.

Bake at 500°F until crusts are golden, about 8 minutes.

Slice pizzas, then top with cilantro and spinach.

Garnish with sun-dried tomato.

Serve with oil and vinegar on side, if desired.

Caramelized Onion And Gorgonzola Pizza Recipe

INGREDIENTS:

2 teaspoons butter

1 large Vidalia onion, thinly sliced

1 teaspoon sugar

1 package (10 ounce size) refrigerated pizza dough

6 ounces Gorgonzola cheese, crumbled

Directions:

In a large saute pan, melt butter over medium heat.

Saute onions in butter until the onions are soft and dark brown, approximately 25 minutes.

Stir in sugar, and continue cooking for 1 or 2 more minutes.

Preheat oven to 425°F (220°C).

Grease a pizza pan or cookie sheet, and press out the dough to desired thickness. Spread onions evenly over the dough, and top with crumbled Gorgonzola.

Bake for 10 to 12 minutes, or until done.

Caramelized Red Onion Pizza Recipe

INGREDIENTS:

1 teaspoon olive oil

3 large red onions, thinly sliced

1 tablespoon maple syrup or light brown sugar.

1 tablespoon balsamic vinegar.

2 tsps.dried basil .

2 cups marinara sauce

pizza dough, rolled into 18- to 19-in. round as needed

4 cups. Swiss chard or spinach, shredded

1/2 cup fresh basil, slivered

1/2 cup low-fat feta cheese, crumbled

1/2 teaspoon dried oregano .

1/4 teaspoon black pepper

Directions:

In large saute pan, heat olive oil over medium heat.

Saute onions, stirring frequently, for about 10 minutes, until caramelized to golden brown.

Stir in maple syrup, vinegar and dried basil then set aside.

Spread marinara sauce over pizza dough, leaving 1/2-in. border.

Arrange Swiss chard on top and top with onions.

Sprinkle with fresh basil, feta cheese, oregano and pepper.

Bake for 30 to 35 minutes at 375ºF until crust is crisp.

Caribbean Pizza Recipe

INGREDIENTS:

1 pizza crust

8 ounces tomato sauce

30 ounces black beans—rinsed and drained

8 ounces crushed pineapple—drained

4 teaspoons lime juice

2 tablespoons fresh cilantro—chopped

6 ounces mozzarella cheese—shredded

Directions:

Preheat oven to 425°F.

Bake crust for 5 minutes.

Spread tomato sauce over partially baked crust.

Top with the black beans and pineapple.

Drizzle the lime juice over the top.

Evenly sprinkle the cilantro and mozzarella cheese on top.

Return to the oven and bake for 12-14 minutes or until edges of crust are turning golden and cheese is melted in the center.

You can make your own crust, use the refrigerated dough, or a pre-made crust like Boboli for this recipe.

If using pre-made, you do not need to partially bake it first unless you want a firmer crust.

Cheese Lovers Pizza Squares Recipe

INGREDIENTS:

    1 can refrigerated pizza dough
    1 cup Ricotta cheese
    8 ounces shredded Mozzarella cheese
    2 plum tomatoes, thinly sliced
    1 cup bell pepper, sliced
    1 teaspoon oregano
    2 tablespoons chopped parsley

Directions:

Preheat oven to 400°F.

Press pizza dough into a 15 x 10-inch jelly roll pan.

Bake for 12 minutes then remove from oven and spread Ricotta cheese over crust. Top with Mozzarella, tomatoes, pepper and oregano.

Return to oven and bake for 6 minutes more or until cheese is melted.

Sprinkle with parsley, cut into squares and serve.

Cheesy Pepper And Mushroom Pizza Recipe

INGREDIENTS:

1 1/2 cup all-purpose flour

1 package active dry yeast

1/4 teaspoon salt

1/2 teaspoon sugar

1 teaspoon cooking oil

Nonstick spray coating

1 tablespoon cornmeal

3/4 cup low-fat cottage cheese, drained

1 egg

2 tablespoons grated Parmesan cheese

1 teaspoon dried basil, crushed

1 clove garlic, minced

1/8 teaspoon pepper

1 medium green or red sweet pepper

1 cup sliced fresh mushrooms

1 cup shredded part-skim mozzarella cheese

Directions:

For crust, mix 3/4 cup of the flour, the yeast, sugar, and salt.

Add oil and 1/2 cup warm water (120ºF to 130ºF).

Beat with electric mixer on low speed 30 seconds, scraping bowl.

Beat on high speed 3 minutes. Stir in as much remaining flour as you can.

Then, knead in enough remaining flour to make a moderately stiff dough that is smooth and elastic (5 minutes total).

Shape into a ball.

Place in a greased bowl; turn once.

Cover; let rise in a warm place until double (about 30 minutes).

Punch down.

Cover then let rest for 10 minutes.

On a floured surface roll dough into a 14-inch circle.

Place on a pizza pan sprayed with nonstick spray coating and sprinkled with the cornmeal.

Build up edges slightly.

Bake crust in a 425°F oven about 10 minutes or until lightly browned.

In a blender container combine cottage cheese, egg, Parmesan, basil, garlic, and pepper.

Cover then blend until smooth.

Spread over hot crust.

Cut green pepper into rings.

Place atop pizza with mushrooms.

Sprinkle with mozzarella.

Bake in a 425°F oven 10 minutes until hot.

Cheesy Pizza Recipe

INGREDIENTS:

1 refrigerated pizza crust

1 1/3 ounce shredded fresh Parmesan cheese

1 tablespoon dried basil

1 cup shredded provolone cheese

1 cup shredded cheddar cheese

1 cup shredded Monterey Jack

1 1/4 cup spaghetti sauce

Directions:

Heat oven to 425ºF degrees.

Grease 12-inch pizza pan or 13 x 9-inch pan.

Unroll dough and place in greased pan and press out with hands forming 1/2 inch rim.

Bake at 425ºF degrees for 7 to 9 minutes or until light golden brown.

Sprinkle partially baked crust with parmesan cheese and basil.

Top with provolone, Cheddar and Monterey Jack cheese.

Drizzle spaghetti sauce over the cheese.

Bake at 425ºF degrees for 12 to 18 minutes or until crust is deep golden brown.

Chicago Style Spinach Pizza Recipe

INGREDIENTS:

1 can (10 oz.) refrigerated pizza crust

1 package (10 oz.) chopped spinach, thawed, well drained

1 package (16 oz.) part-skim mozzarella cheese, shredded

1/4 cup (1 oz.) Parmesan cheese, shredded, divided

1 can (28 oz.) tomatoes, drained, cut up

2 garlic cloves, minced

2 teaspoons dried oregano leaves

1/2 teaspoon red pepper flakes, optional

Directions:

Heat oven to 500ºF.

Press pizza crust onto bottom and sides of well greased 10 inch deep dish pizza pan or 9 x 13 inch baking dish.

Mix spinach, mozzarella cheese and 2 tablespoons Parmesan.

Spread evenly over crust.

Mix tomatoes, garlic, oregano and pepper flakes.

Spread over cheese mixture.

Sprinkle with remaining 2 tablespoons Parmesan cheese.

Bake 10 minutes.

Reduce heat to 375ºF and bake for an additional 20 minutes.

Classic Cheese Pizza Recipe

INGREDIENTS:

1 ounce fresh yeast

or

1/2 ounce dried yeast

1 pinch sugar

1/2 pint lukewarm water

14 ounces plain flour

1 teaspoon salt (scant)

1/4 pint olive oil

corn meal (polenta)

3/4 pint tomato and garlic sauce

1 pound mozzarella, cut into 1/4 inch dice

6 tablespoons Parmesan, freshly grated

Directions:

Crumble the fresh yeast or sprinkle the dried yeast and a pinch of sugar into 3 tablespoons of lukewarm water. Be sure that the water is lukewarm (110 - 115°F. - neither too hot nor too cold to the touch).

Let it stand for 2 to 3 minutes, then stir the yeast and sugar into the water until completely dissolved.

Put the cup in a warm, draught-free place for 3 to 5 minutes, until the yeast bubbles up and the mixture almost doubles in volume.

If the yeast does not bubble, start over again with fresh yeast.

Sift the flour and salt into a large, warmed bowl.

Make a well in the centre of the flour and pour in the yeast mixture, 3/8 pint of lukewarm water and 3 tablespoons of the olive oil.

Mix the dough with a fork or your fingers.

When you can gather it into a rough ball, place the dough on a floured board and knead it for about 15 minutes, until smooth, shiny and elastic.

Dust the dough lightly with flour, put in a large clean bowl and cover.

Place the bowl in a warm, draught-free spot for about 1 1/2 hours, until the dough has doubled in bulk.

Now preheat the oven to 450°F.

Punch the dough down with your fists and break off about one quarter of it to make the first of the 4 pizzas.

Knead the small piece on a floured board or a table for a minute or so, working in a little flour if the dough seems sticky.

Flatten the ball into a circle about 1 inch thick with the palm of your hand.

Hold the circle in your hands and stretch the dough by turning the circle and pulling your hands apart gently at the same time.

When the circle is about 7 or 8 inches across, spread it out on the floured board again and pat it smooth, pressing together any tears in the dough.

Then roll the dough with a rolling pin, from the centre to the far edge, turning it clockwise after each roll, until you have a circle of pastry about 10 inches across and about 1/8 inch thick.

Crimp or flute the edge of the circle with your thumbs until it forms a little rim.

Dust a large baking sheet lightly with corn meal and gently place the pizza dough on top of it.

Knead, stretch and roll the rest of the dough into 3 more pizzas.

Pour 6 tablespoons of the tomato sauce on each pizza and spread it with a pastry brush or the back of a spoon.

To make a cheese pizza, sprinkle the sauce with 6 tablespoons of mozzarella and 2 tablespoons of grated Parmesan.

Dribble 2 tablespoons of olive oil over the pizza and bake it on the lowest shelf or the floor of the oven.

Reduce the oven temperature to 400°F after 5 minutes and cook for about 10 minutes in all, until the crust is lightly browned and the filling bubbling hot.

Cold Vegetable Pizza Recipe

INGREDIENTS:

16 ounces cream cheese—softened

1 cup mayonnaise

1 Envelope Hidden Valley Ranch Dressing

1 package refrigerated crescent rolls

1/2 cup chopped celery

1/2 cup chopped cauliflower

1/2 cup black olives

Directions:

Preheat oven to 350ºF degrees.

Press out crescent rolls in a jelly roll pan and bake for 8 to 10 minutes.

Mix together the cream cheese, mayonnaise and Hidden Valley Ranch Dressing.

Pour on top of cooled crescents.

Spread the chopped vegetables over pan and top with shredded cheese.

Chill several hours or overnight

Corn And Tomato Pizza Recipe

INGREDIENTS:

1 pizza crust

1 1/2 cup frozen corn—thawed

1 1/2 cup plum tomatoes—seeded and chopped

1/4 cup chopped fresh basil

3 cloves garlic—minced

1 teaspoon dried oregano leaves

1/2 teaspoon coarse ground black pepper

2 tablespoons dijon mustard—optional

1 cup shredded mozzarella cheese

2 tablespoons grated parmesan cheese

Directions:

Prepare pizza crust.

Preheat oven to 450°F.

Combine corn, tomatoes, basil, garlic, oregano and pepper in medium bowl.

Spread mustard over prepared crust, if desired.

Sprinkle crust with mozzarella cheese and top with corn mixture and Parmesan cheese.

Bake 18 to 20 minutes or until crust is golden brown and cheese is melted.

Cut into wedges.

Double Filled Mushroom Pizza Recipe

INGREDIENTS:

Filling 1

1/2 cup stuffed olives—sliced

4 ounces sliced canned mushrooms

Filling 2

5 small scallions—thinly sliced

Pizza:

1 Loaf French Bread Loaf—14" long

1 Jar Pizza Sauce

1 cup Mozzarella Cheese—shredded

Directions:

Preheat oven to 350ºF degrees.

Slice bread vertically into 10 slices without cutting completely through the bread. Spoon sauce equally into each section.

Alternate fillings between slices.

Sprinkle cheese over fillings.

Loosely wrap pizza in heavy aluminum foil.

Bake 30 minutes, or until heated through.

Open foil and bake again another 10 to 15 minutes.

www.crueltyfreeorganics.net[1] For all your organic herbs,spices and oils.

---

1. http://www.crueltyfreeorganics.net/

PIZZA BASES

Whole Wheat Pizza Crust Recipe

Ingredients:

1 teaspoon white sugar

1 1/2 cup warm water (110ºF/45ºC)

1 tablespoon active dry yeast

1 tablespoon olive oil

1 teaspoon salt

2 cups whole wheat flour

1 1/2 cup all-purpose flour

Directions:

In a large bowl, dissolve sugar in warm water.

Sprinkle yeast over the top, and let stand for about 10 minutes, until foamy.

Stir the olive oil and salt into the yeast mixture, then mix in the whole wheat flour and 1 cup of the all-purpose flour until dough starts to come together.

Tip dough out onto a surface floured with the remaining all-purpose flour, and knead until all of the flour has been absorbed, and the ball of dough becomes smooth, about 10 minutes.

Place dough in an oiled bowl, and turn to coat the surface.

Cover loosely with a towel, and let stand in a warm place until doubled in size, about 1 hour.

When the dough is doubled, tip the dough out onto a lightly floured surface, and divide into 2 pieces for 2 thin crust, or leave whole to make one thick crust.

Form into a tight ball.

Let rise for about 45 minutes, until doubled.

Preheat the oven to 425°F (220°C).

Roll a ball of dough with a rolling pin until it will not stretch any further.

Then, drape it over both of your fists, and gently pull the edges outward, while rotating the crust.

When the circle has reached the desired size, place on a well oiled pizza pan.

Top pizza with your favorite toppings (sauce, cheese,or vegetables).

Bake for 16 to 20 minutes (depending on thickness) in the preheated oven, until the crust is crisp and golden at the edges, and cheese is melted on the top.

Basic Pizza Dough Recipe

INGREDIENTS:

2 packages dry yeast

1 1/2 cup lukewarm water

4 cups flour

1 teaspoon salt

1/2 teaspoon sugar

1 tablespoon olive oil

Directions:

Dissolve yeast in water; set aside for 5 minutes, stirring occasionally.

Combine flour, salt, sugar and oil in bowl and make a well in the center.

When water/yeast mixture is bubbly, pour into the center of the well.

Start kneading dough, bringing flour toward center of bowl gradually increasing the kneading motion.

If dough feels dry, add a little more water; if it feels sticky, add more flour.

Knead vigorously until dough is smooth and elastic.

Roll into ball; cover with a damp cloth. Let rest for about 20 minutes in warm place.

Beat dough with your palm to expel gas formed while fermenting.

Roll dough again into ball and place in greased bowl.

Baste with oil.

Cover with plastic wrap and; store in the refrigerator.

When ready to use, place dough on floured counter top or table.

Flatten with your hands, working from center out (a rolling pin may do also).

Push dough evenly onto greased cookie sheet or pizza pan, forming a 12-inch circle with edges thicker than middle.

Apply favorite topping in desired amounts.
Bake in hot oven (475ºF to 500ºF degrees) until golden brown.

Basic Pizza Dough Recipe 1

INGREDIENTS:

4 1/2 cups unbleached all-purpose white flour

1 teaspoon salt

1/4 cup olive oil

2 packages dry yeast

1 1/2 cup Warm water

2 teaspoons light brown sugar

Directions:

Measure 1/2 cup warm water (110°F) into 2 cup container and stir in the brown sugar. (Make sure water is warm, not hot, too hot will kill the yeast).

Dissolve the 2 packages of dried yeast in the water and set it aside for 5 minutes. Will become frothy. (about 2 cups worth!)

Sift 4 cups of the flour and the salt into a large mixing bowl.

Make a depression in the middle of the flour and pour in 3/4 of the olive oil and 1 cup of warm water.

When the yeast is ready, add it also.

Dust your kneading surface with flour, then mix the ingredients in the bowl with your hands.

Place dough ball on the floured surface and knead from 8 to 10 minutes.

Add flour to the kneading surface if the dough is too sticky or wet.

Eventually the dough will become elastic.

Rub the insides of a clean bowl with the remaining olive oil and place the dough in it, coating the dough with olive oil by turning it in the bowl.

Cover with a clean cloth and let rise in warm, draft- free place until double in size, 1 1/2 hours to 2 hours.

An oven with the light on or a lit burner pilot will provide suitable heat for rising dough.

When dough has risen, divide into two halves, then roll each out on floured surface.

A round shape may be cut out with table knife using 12" bowl or plate as template.

Basic Pizza Dough Recipe 2

INGREDIENTS:

3 1/4 cups unbleached flour

2 teaspoons salt

1 cup warm water

1 envelope active dry yeast

3 tablespoons olive oil

Directions:

In a bowl, combine the flour and salt, and mix thoroughly.

In a separate stainless steel bowl, combine the water and yeast, and using a whisk, add 2 tablespoons of oil.

Let rest for 5 minutes.

Pour the water into the center of the flour, and with a spatula, stir to combine well into a sticky mass.

Pour this mass out onto a lightly floured surface and begin to knead the dough by working the dough with the heel of the palm of your hand.

Push outward and pull the inside edge over the top.

Repeat the process over again to create a smooth ball of dough free of stickiness. Place the ball of dough into a clean stainless steel bowl that has been brushed with the remaining 1 tablespoon of olive oil.

Cover with a clean cloth and let rise at room temperature for 1 1/2 hours or until it has doubled in size.

When the dough has risen it can be divided in half and the two pieces formed into two balls which will later be patted into the traditional pizza shape

Boboli Pizza Crust Recipe

INGREDIENTS:

1 package dry yeast

1/4 cup water

2 1/4 cups warm water

6 tablespoons olive oil, + extra for pans

6 cups flour

1 teaspoon salt

Directions:

Dissolve yeast in warm water (105°F is perfect).

Let it sit for two minutes.

Add the rest of the ingredients and mix well.

Turn out onto board and knead for ten minutes.

Place back in bowl covered with a damp towel and let rise 30 to 40 minutes.

Divide dough into 3 parts and place in 3 olive-oiled pie pans.

Dimple dough with fingers.

Place on top the following mixture:

Coarse sea (or Kosher) salt, fresh ground pepper, chopped rosemary and thyme.

If herbs are dried, soak them in water for 10 minutes and then pat dry on paper towels.

Let rise 50 to 60 minutes.

Bake at 350°F for 25 minutes.

May dip in olive oil.

Boboli Type Pizza Crust Recipe (Breadmaker Recipe)

INGREDIENTS:

1 cup water

3 cups all purpose flour

1 teaspoon salt

2 tablespoons olive oil

1 tablespoon sugar

2 teaspoons active dry yeast

1 teaspoon minced garlic

2 teaspoons parmesan cheese

1/2 teaspoon Italian seasoning

Parmesan cheese to sprinkle

Directions:

Add all ingredients except the second lot of parmesan cheese to the breadmaker in the order listed by your manufacturer.

It is a good idea to put the garlic down inside the flour so it does not slow the yeast. Set breadmaker on dough setting.

When complete, form two crusts on pizza pans, sprinkle with parmesan cheese, cover and let rise again.

Bake 5-10 minutes at about 450ºF until light brown.

Cool.

Wrap tightly in foil and freeze until you you need to cook the pizza/s.

Classic Pizza Crust Recipe

INGREDIENTS:

1 package active dry yeast

2 1/2 cups sifted flour

1 teaspoon salt

1 cup warm water

1 tablespoon cooking oil

Directions:

In a large mixing bowl, combine the yeast, 1 cup of flour, and the salt.

Mix.

Next, add the water and oil.

Beat on low speed for 30 seconds.

Scrape the sides of the bowl and continue to beat on high speed for 3 minutes.

By hand, stir in enough flour to make the dough stiff.

Knead until smooth which can take up to 10 minutes.

Place in a well greased bowl and turn the dough until it is lightly greased.

Cover and let rise for about 1 1/2 hours or until the dough has doubled in size.

Punch it down and chill for 2 hours.

Cut the dough in half.

On a floured surface, roll the halves into 12 inch circle and about 1/8 inch thick. Brush the surfaces of the dough with olive oil and add the toppings of your choice. Cook at 425ºF for 25 minutes.

Cornmeal Pizza Crust Recipe (Breadmaker Recipe)

INGREDIENTS:

1 cup warm water

1/4 teaspoon salt—optional

2 1/2 cups all-purpose flour—divided

1 cup cornmeal—plus

1 tablespoon cornmeal—divided

2 tablespoons sugar or honey

2 teaspoons active dry yeast

Directions:

Measure carefully, placing all ingredients except 1 tablespoon cornmeal in bread machine pan in order specified by owner's manual.

Program basic dough cycle setting and then press start.

Remove dough from bread machine pan and let it rest 2 to 3 minutes.

Pat and gently stretch dough into 14- to 15-inch circle.

Spray a 14-inch pizza pan with nonstick cooking spray; sprinkle with remaining 1 tablespoon cornmeal.

Press dough into pan.

Follow topping and baking directions for individual recipes.

One 14 inch crust makes 8 servings

Deep Dish Pizza Crust Recipe

INGREDIENTS:

3 cups all-purpose flour

1/8 cup olive oil

2 jumbo eggs—room temperature

2 tablespoons thyme

1 cup warm water

1 package rapid rise yeast

2 teaspoons sugar

Directions:

Whisk together water, yeast and sugar in a bowl and set aside to proof for 10 minutes. In a large bowl sift together flour and salt and sprinkle in thyme.

Mix eggs into yeast mixture.

Pour liquid into dry ingredients and mix until a soft sticky dough forms.

Remove dough to a lightly floured surface and knead 5 minutes, until dough is no longer sticky.

Place in a well oiled bowl, turning to coat all sides, cover and allow to rise until doubled in bulk 2 - 3 hours.

Punch dough down and place into a well oiled 12" pizza pan.

Using your hands, move dough around the bottom of the pan and 2/3 the way up the sides.

Set aside and let rise 10 minutes.

Brush crust lightly with olive oil and add toppings.

Easy Pizza Dough Recipe

INGREDIENTS:

3 1/2 cups unbleached, all-purpose flour

2 packages dry active yeast

1 teaspoon salt

1/2 teaspoon sugar

1 1/2 cup lukewarm water from the tap

1/2 teaspoon olive oil

Flour, for the work surface

Cornmeal, to dust

Directions:

In a mixing bowl fitted with a dough hook, place flour, yeast, salt and sugar.

While mixer is running, gradually add water and knead on low speed until dough is firm and smooth, about 10 minutes.

Turn machine off.

Pour oil down inside of bowl.

Turn on low once more for 15 seconds to coat inside of bowl and all surfaces of dough with the oil.

Cover bowl with plastic wrap.

Let dough rise in warm spot until doubled in bulk, about 2 hours.

Preheat oven to 500°F.

If using a pizza stone, place stone in oven on bottom rack, preheat oven 1 hour ahead. Punch dough down, cut in half.

Place half of the dough on generously floured work surface.

By hand, form dough loosely into a ball and stretch into a circle.

Using floured rolling pin, roll dough into large circle until very thin. Don't worry if your circle isn't perfect and if you get a hole just pinch the edges back together.

To prevent dough from sticking to counter, turn over the dough and sprinkle with flour.

Also, flour the counter top and rolling pin as needed.

Sprinkle pizza peel or cookie sheet generously with cornmeal.

Transfer dough to pizza peel or cookie sheet with no lip.

Add toppings.

Slide dough onto pizza stone or place cookie sheet with pizza on bottom rack.

Bake 10 to 12 minutes or until golden.

Roll out remaining dough and top with desired toppings or freeze in freezer bags.

Heart Shaped Pizza Recipe

INGREDIENTS:

1 cup water

2 tablespoons milk

2 teaspoons sugar

1 1/4 teaspoon salt

1 tablespoon butter

1 tablespoon olive oil

1 tablespoon durum semolina (or corn meal)

1 cup unbleached all-purpose flour

2 cups unbleached bread flour

1 1/4 teaspoon yeast

Directions:

Food Processor:

Place water, milk, sugar, salt, butter and olive oil in bowl of food processor and pulse to dissolve sugar and salt.

Add yeast, semolina or corn meal, bread flour and all purpose flour.

Process until a soft ball forms.

Remove from machine and allow to rest, covered with a towel, about 45 minutes.

OR to make by hand:

Use only all-purpose flour.

Place water, milk, sugar, salt, butter and olive oil in bowl and dissolve sugar and salt.

Stir in yeast, semolina or corn meal, all purpose flour and knead to form a soft, but not-too sticky dough (8-10 minutes).

Allow to rest, covered with a towel about 45 minutes.

Deflate dough very gently before using and allow it to rest 15 minutes more before using in a recipe.

You may refrigerate dough in an oiled plastic bag for up to two days.

Shape dough into a heart.

Top with your favorite sauce and toppings.

Bake in a hot oven 425 - 450°F. for 15 - 20 minutes.

Herb Pizza Dough Recipe

INGREDIENTS:

1 package active dry yeast

1 teaspoon sugar

7/8 cup warm water—110ºF

1/4 cup Italian seasoning

2 1/4 cups flour

1 tablespoon flour

1/2 teaspoon salt

1 tablespoon garlic olive oil—as needed

Oil And cornmeal for pan

Directions:

Stir together the yeast,sugar and warm water.

Let stand until foamy, about 10 minutes.

In the work bowl of a food processor fitted with the steel blade, chop the herbs.

Turn off machine.

Add flour and salt.

Turn the machine on and off a couple of times.

While the machine is running, add yeast.

Process until the dough forms a ball at the side of the bowl.

Add garlic olive oil and process for 30 to 40 seconds more.

Transfer dough to a bowl that has been oiled with olive oil.

Turn the dough until the entire surface has been coated with the oil.

Cover bowl with a damp towel and allow to rise in a warm draft free place for 1 hour or until doubled.

Roll out on a lightly floured surface and if dough is too elastic, try tossing it from hand to hand to flatten it out.

Lightly grease the pizza pan with a little oil and sprinkle with cornmeal.

Place the dough on the pizza pan and trim the edges.
Bake for 10 minutes at 425°F.
Remove from oven, lightly brush the crust with a little more oil.
Top as desired.
Makes enough dough for one 12" crust.

Pizza Dough Recipe (Breadmaker)

INGREDIENTS:

1 1/2 teaspoon bread machine yeast

3 cups all-purpose flour

3/4 cup milk

2 tablespoons olive oil

1/2 cup lukewarm water

1 1/2 teaspoon salt

Pinch of sugar

Directions:

Place all ingredients except water in a food processor.

Pulse to mix well.

Then turn machine on and drizzle the water in until it forms a ball. Let the ball go around a few times in the machine to knead it a bit.

Remove dough onto a floured surface and knead well for a few minutes until elastic.

Place in a greased bowl and let rise until doubled.

Remove from bowl and punch down.

Cut into 2 pieces and roll out into 4 medium size crusts, enough to feed 4 people. Turn oven on and preheat at 400°F for 30 minutes, if using pizza stone.

If no stone, preheat oven to 400°F for 10-15 minutes.

Place pizza crust on the back of a baking sheet that has been covered with a sprinkling of cornmeal.

Place in oven and bake for 8 minutes.

Remove and cover with toppings.

Place back in oven and bake for 8 more minutes until crust is golden and cheese is bubbly.

New York Style Pizza Dough Recipe

INGREDIENTS:

1 1/2 cup warm water

2 1/2 teaspoons granulated sugar

2 1/2 teaspoons salt

1 tablespoon olive oil

4 1/2 cups all-purpose flour

1/2 teaspoon active dry yeast

1/2 cup cornmeal

Sauce, cheese, and toppings of your choice

Directions:

In a large bowl, dissolve sugar and salt in water.

Add oil and flour to bowl and stir with heavy spoon for 1 minute.

Turn dough out onto a lightly floured surface and press into a circle.

Sprinkle yeast evenly over dough and knead for 12 minutes.

Divide dough into portions:

4 equal portions for calzones

3 equal portions for 8" pizzas

2 equal portions for 12" pizzas.

Place dough balls in a bowl, cover with plastic wrap, and allow to rise for 1 1/2 hours in a warm location.

Place a dough ball on a lightly floured surface and sprinkle a light coating of flour on top.

Working from the edges to the center, press dough into a circle.

Preheat a pizza stone in a 500°F oven for 1 hour.

Coat a large cutting board with cornmeal and place the flattened dough onto the cornmeal.

Spread sauce over crust and top with cheese and desired toppings.

Gently shake the cutting board from side to side, assuring it isn't sticking to the board.

For a calzone, fold the crust over in half.

Slide the pizza/calzone from the cutting board directly onto the stone in the oven. Bake in 500°F oven for 20-25 minutes, until crust is golden.

New York-Style Pizza Crust Recipe 2 (Breadmaker Recipe)

INGREDIENTS:

2/3 cup warm water

1/2 teaspoon salt

2 1/4 cups all-purpose flour

1 teaspoon sugar

2 teaspoons active dry yeast

1 tablespoon cornmeal—optional

Directions:

Measure carefully, placing all ingredients except cornmeal in bread machine pan in order specified by owner's manual.

Program dough cycle setting then press start.

Remove dough from bread machine pan and let rest 2 to 3 minutes.

Pat and gently stretch dough from edges until dough seems to not stretch anymore. Let rest 2 to 3 minutes more.

Continue patting and stretching until dough is 12 to 14 inches in diameter.

Spray a 12 to 14 inch pizza pan with cooking spray and sprinkle with cornmeal, if desired.

Press dough into pan.

Preheat oven to 450°F.

Follow topping and baking directions for individual recipes, baking pizza on bottom rack of oven.

Pizza Crust Recipe

INGREDIENTS:

0.47 L warm water (110ºF - 115ºF)

59 milliliters olive oil

2 packages yeast

1 2/5 L all-purpose flour

9 9/10 milliliters of salt yellow cornmeal

Directions:

Proof yeast with salt in warm water.

Mix yeast, water and olive oil, stir in flour 1 cup at a time.

Turn out onto floured surface, knead until smooth for 5 to 7 minutes adding flour as necessary.

Dough will be soft.

Place in oiled bowl, turning to coat all sides, cover with plastic wrap and let rise in warm place until doubled.

Punch down and let rest 15 mins.

Divide in half and press out into two 12 inch round pizza pans or 10x15x1 pans or 1 of each sprinkled with yellow cornmeal (prevents crust from sticking).

Pizza Dough (Breadmaker Recipe)

INGREDIENTS:

1 cup water

2 tablespoons water

2 tablespoons oil

3 cups bread flour

1 teaspoon sugar

1 teaspoon salt

2 1/2 teaspoons active dry yeast

Directions:

Place ingredients in pan in order listed or as directed per machine instructions.

Select white dough cycle.

Makes two 12 inch regular crusts or one 16 inch deep dish crust.

Top with desired toppings and bake at 400°F for 18-20 minutes or until crust is light brown.

Pizza Dough Recipe 2

INGREDIENTS:

3/4 tablespoon yeast

1 1/2 cup water

1 1/2 teaspoon salt

3 tablespoons oil

4 cups flour

Directions:

Dissolve yeast in water (You can add a pinch of sugar).

Stir in salt, oil and half of flour.

Gradually add remaining flour, mixing well.

Knead 8-10 minutes or until smooth and elastic.

Place in greased bowl and let rise until double (1/2-1 hour).

Punch down and let rise again until double.

Punch down and divide.

Pan out on pizza pans.

Top with pizza sauce & toppings.

Bake at 400ºF for 20-25 minutes.

Polenta Pizza Crust Recipe

INGREDIENTS:

1 tablespoon active dry yeast

1 tablespoon barley malt extract

1 cup warm water

3/4 cup semolina

1 cup unbleached all purpose flour

3/4 cup polenta/corn meal

1 teaspoon salt

3 tablespoons extra virgin olive oil

Directions:

In a large bowl or electric mixer, dissolve the yeast and barley malt in warm water. Add the semolina, flour, polenta, salt, and olive oil. Combine well.

Knead the dough until it is shiny and smooth, adding flour as needed.

Place the dough in a lightly oiled bowl, cover with plastic wrap and let rise until doubled, about 2 hours.

When dough has risen, punch down and roll out to a large circle and transfer to a baking sheet or pizza pan.

Top with any preferred topping and bake in a preheated 425ºF oven for 20 - 25 minutes.

This is good topped with roasted vegetables.

Pourable Pizza Crust Recipe

INGREDIENTS:

3 tablespoons nstant active dry yeast

Warm water (110°F)(just enough to dissolve the active yeast)

7 pounds all-purpose or bread flour

1 package (1 lb 2 1/2 oz.) Instant nonfat dry milk

8 3/4 ounces sugar

1 1/4 teaspoon salt

1/8 cup olive oil

Cornmeal

Directions:

Dissolve dry yeast in warm water.

Let stand 5 minutes.

Place flour, milk, sugar, and salt in mixer bowl.

Using a whip, blend on low speed for 8 minutes.

Add dissolved yeast and oil.

Blend on medium speed for 10 minutes. Batter will be lumpy.

Oil three sheet pans (18" x26" x1").

Sprinkle each pan with 1 oz (approximately 3 Tbsp) cornmeal.

Pour or spread 3 lb 6 oz (1 1/2 quart) batter into each pan.

Let stand for 25 minutes.

Bake until crust is set: Conventional Oven: 475 degrees F, 10 minutes. Convection Oven: 425°F, 7 minutes.

Top each prebaked crust with desired topping.

Bake until heated through and cheese is melted:

Conventional Oven: 475°F, 10-15 minutes. Convection Oven: 425°F, 5 minutes.

Soft Pizza Dough Recipe

INGREDIENTS:

1 frozen loaf bread dough

Directions:

Allow dough to defrost.

Roll out to fit pan.

Bake until crust is set

Conventional Oven: 475°F for 10 minutes. Convection Oven: 425°F for 7 minutes.

Thin Crust Pizza Dough Recipe

INGREDIENTS:

3 cups bread flour

7/8 cup warm water

1 tablespoon vegetable shortening

1 teaspoon active dry yeast

1 teaspoon salt

1/2 teaspoon sugar

Directions:

In a heavy-duty stand mixer fitted with dough hook, add the water, shortening, yeast, and sugar.

Mix thoroughly until yeast has fully dissolved.

Add flour and salt.

Mix on low until most of the flour and water has mixed, then continue kneading for 10 minutes. The dough will be loose and scrappy at first and will eventually form a cohesive ball. There should be no raw flour or crumbs remaining in the bowl. The dough should be somewhat dry and dense.

Place the dough ball into a large bowl and cover tightly with plastic wrap. Let the dough rise for 24 hours in the refrigerator before using.

Preheat your oven to 500°F about one hour before you plan to bake the pizza.

Turn the dough out onto a large surface and dust with flour.

Using a heavy rolling pin, roll the dough out very thin to form a 24-inch or larger circle. If you're using a cutter pizza pan (recommended), dust the pan lightly with flour, place the dough in the pan and dock.

Use the rolling pin to trim off the excess dough drooping over the sides of the pan.

If you wish to cook the pizza directly on a pizza stone (not using a pan), then place the dough on a dusted pizza-peel, dock, and fold the edge over 1-inch all the way around and pinch it up to form a raised lip or rim.

Next, precook the crust for 4 minutes before adding any sauce or toppings.

Remove the crust from the oven and pop any large air pockets that may have formed.

Add your sauce, shredded mozzarella cheese, and your favorite toppings.

Continue baking, rotating the pan half way through so that it cooks evenly, until crust is sufficiently browned and crisp, about 10 to 15 minutes.

Remove the pizza from the oven and slide pizza out of cooking pan onto a large wire cooling rack or cutting board.

Allow to cool for 5 minutes before transferring to a serving pan. This step allows the crust to stay crisp while it cools, otherwise the trapped steam will soften the crust. Once cool, use a pizza cutter to slice the pie into pieces and enjoy!

Whole Wheat Pizza Crust Recipe 2 (Breadmaker Recipe)

INGREDIENTS:

1 1/4 cup warm water

1/4 teaspoon salt (optional)

2 tablespoons honey or sugar

2 cups all-purpose flour,sifted

1 cup whole wheat flour

2 teaspoons active dry yeast

1 tablespoon cornmeal

Directions:

Measure carefully, placing all ingredients except cornmeal in bread machine pan in order specified by owner's manual.

Program dough cycle setting and press start.

Remove dough from bread machine pan and let it rest 2 to 3 minutes.

Pat and gently stretch dough into 14- to 15-inch circle.

Spray 14-inch pizza pan with nonstick cooking spray then sprinkle with cornmeal, if desired.

Press dough into pan.

Follow topping and baking directions for individual recipes.

One thick 14-inch crust is 8 servings.

www.crueltyfreeorganics.net[1] For all your organic herbs,spices and oils

---

1. http://www.crueltyfreeorganics.net/

PIZZA SAUCES

Authentic Homemade Pizza Sauce Recipe

Ingredients:

1 medium onion, finely chopped

2 tablespoons olive oil

500 grams can whole/chopped Italian plum tomatoes

2 teaspoons concentrated tomato puree

1 tablespoon white wine vinegar

3 teaspoons sugar

Directions:

In a large saucepan, gently saute the onion in the oil until transparent.

Add the tomatoes and bring to the boil.

Once simmering, add the tomato puree, the vinegar and sugar.

Simmer for a full hour, using a wooden spoon to break up any tomato pieces.

If the sauce still has pieces of tomato, pass through a sieve before bottling and storing in the refrigerator for up to two weeks.

Spread thinly on pizza, use over pasta with a grated, strong, hard cheese, or use as a base for more complex sauces for pasta.

Basic Pizza Sauce Recipe

INGREDIENTS:

35 ounces canned whole tomatoes

1 teaspoon basil

1 clove garlic, peeled & crushed

2 tablespoons tomato paste

Salt and pepper to taste

Directions:

Pour the contents of the tomato can into a 2-quart, heavy non-aluminum saucepan and coarsely crush the tomatoes with a fork.

Add the herbs, garlic, tomato paste, salt, and pepper.

Bring to a bubble over medium heat, stirring to mix the seasonings.

As soon as the sauce begins to bubble, turn the heat to low and maintain the sauce at a gentle simmer.

Cook, uncovered, stirring from occasionally, for a minimum of 15 minutes and a maximum of 1 hour.

Firehouse Pizza Sauce Recipe

INGREDIENTS:

1 (6 ounce) can tomato paste

3/4 cup warm water (110ºF/45ºC)

3 tablespoons grated Parmesan cheese

1 teaspoon minced garlic

1 tablespoon honey

3/4 teaspoon onion powder

1/4 teaspoon dried oregano

1/4 teaspoon dried marjoram

1/4 teaspoon dried basil

1/4 teaspoon ground black pepper

1/8 teaspoon cayenne pepper

1/8 teaspoon dried red pepper flakes

Salt to taste

Directions:

In a small bowl, combine tomato paste, water, Parmesan cheese, garlic, honey, onion powder, oregano, marjoram, basil, ground black pepper, cayenne pepper, red pepper flakes and salt.

Mmix together, breaking up any clumps of cheese.

Sauce should sit for 30 minutes to blend.

Spread over pizza dough and prepare pizza as desired.

Onion & Garlic Sauce Recipe

INGREDIENTS:

1/2 onion, minced

1 or more cloves garlic, finely minced

2 tablespoons olive or vegetable oil (more if needed)

1 can tomato sauce (16 oz.)

1 can tomato paste (6 oz.)

2 teaspoons sugar (optional) it takes out the bitterness of the tomato

1 teaspoon basil - dried

1 teaspoon oregano - dried

1/2 teaspoon salt

Directions:

Mince onion and garlic.

Saute in olive oil until onion is clear and tender.

Add rest of the ingredients to skillet and simmer for 15-20 minutes.

Makes enough sauce for 2 pizzas.

Pizza Sauce Recipe

INGREDIENTS:

- 1 can (15 oz.) tomato sauce
- 1 tablespoon oregano
- 1 tablespoon basil
- 1 teaspoon garlic powder
- 1/2 teaspoon onion powder
- 2 tablespoons brown sugar, if desired
- 1 teaspoon salt
- 1/2 teaspoon pepper

Directions:

Combine ingredients in a small saucepan and cook over low heat.

Spread on two pizza crusts

Top with favorite toppings.

Pizza Sauce Recipe 2

INGREDIENTS:

1 large onion

2 cloves garlic

1 teaspoon tomato puree (tomato paste)

1 can (14 oz size) chopped tomatoes

Seasoning

Directions:

Chop onion and garlic, microwave for five minutes (omit this step if you don't have a microwave; it isn't essential but it makes the sauce quicker to cook).

Transfer to saucepan, add tomato puree and stir.

Add tinned tomatoes.

Season, bring to boil, and simmer for about 15-20 minutes until it has reduced to a jammy consistency.

For seasoning use salt, freshly milled black pepper, Worcestershire like sauce and some sort of herbs; fresh basil if you have it, or dried Italian seasoning.

Pizza Sauce Recipe 3

INGREDIENTS:

3 tablespoons olive oil

3 cloves garlic, minced

28 ounces can whole cooked tomatoes

1 tablespoon dried oregano

1 teaspoon dried basil

Salt and pepper to taste

Directions:

Warm olive oil with garlic on medium heat.

Stir and cook for 2 to 3 minutes.

Add drained and seeded tomatoes along with salt, pepper, oregano and basil then stir and cook for 15-20 minutes until thick enough to spread over pizza dough.

Pizza Sauce Recipe 4

INGREDIENTS:

2 cans (6 ounce) tomato paste

2 cloves garlic

3 tablespoons dried parsley flakes

4 teaspoons dried onion flakes

1 teaspoon dried oregano

1 teaspoon dried basil

2 cups water

Directions:

Combine tomato paste, garlic, parsley flakes, onion, oregano, basil and water in 2 quart saucepan.

Cook over medium high heat until mixture boils.

Reduce heat to low and simmer 10 minutes.

Cool slightly and spread on pizza crust

Top as desired and bake.

South Beach Diet Simple Pizza Sauce Recipe

Ingredients:

1 tablespoon tomato paste

1 cup tomato puree

1/8 teaspoon crushed red pepper flakes

2 teaspoons dried oregano

2 teaspoons dried basil

2 teaspoons dried thyme

Directions:

Combine all in small saucepan and cook over low heat for 15 minutes, or until sauce thickens.

White Pizza Sauce Recipe

Ingredients:
6 tablespoons butter
6 tablespoons olive oil
2 tablespoons white wine
1 teaspoon rosemary
1 teaspoon basil
2 cloves garlic; minced

Directions:
Saute garlic in butter and olive oil.
Add all other ingredients and simmer for 15 minutes.

White Pizza Sauce Recipe 2

Ingredients:
1/3 cup flour
3/4 teaspoon salt
1/8 teaspoon pepper
1/8 teaspoon paprika
1/8 teaspoon onion powder
2 cups milk
1 tablespoon butter

Directions:
Put the first 5 ingredients in a saucepan.
Gradually whisk in milk until no lumps remain.
Heat and stir until boiling and thickened.
Stir in butter until melted.
Spread on pizza crust
Top with favorite toppings.

Bon Appetit

For all your organic herbs,spices and oils.

www.crueltyfreeorganics.net[1]

(Images shown in this ebook are for decorative purposes only. They are not meant to represent any particular pizza, recipe or products mentioned in the text)

Also by Neil Milliner

TheFreeMans Poetry Book
And So The Journey Begins
Artful Dwellings: Making Your House a Home With Beautiful Art
Art In The Workplace: Fostering Creativity and Innovation
E-commerce SEO Strategies: Selling Online Successfully
Delicious Vegetarian Pizzas For Everybody
I'm Married. Now What?: What To Do After "I Do!"
The Train Of Life